STUDY GUIDE

WHEN TROUBLE COMES

JIM BERG

When Trouble Comes Study Guide
Jim Berg

Design and page layout by Stouffer Designs

© 2024 by Hope & Help Ministries, LLC
First Edition © 2004 BJU Press
Second Edition © 2024 Hope & Help Ministries, LLC
Greenville, South Carolina

JimBerg.com

Printed in the United States of America
All rights reserved

ISBN 9798218415655

15 14 13 12 11 10 9 8 7 6 5 4 3 2 1

TABLE OF CONTENTS

Introduction 1

Week 1 . . . . . The Danger 2

Week 2 . . . . The Deliverance . . . 20

Week 3 . . . . The Display 36

Week 4 . . . . The Delight 52

Introduction

Wise people prepare for any crisis they see on the horizon.

Coastal dwellers in my home state of South Carolina quickly move into an "emergency preparedness" mode when they are informed that a hurricane is brewing in the Atlantic and will make landfall within a few days or hours.

They board up windows, move outdoor furniture inside, remove valuables, and work feverishly until the last possible moment when they have to vacate the dwelling themselves and move to safety further inland.

Though everyone within hurricane-prone regions knows that the potential of a threatening storm exists, not everyone takes the necessary precautions that will preserve as much property and life as possible. Some people are ignorant of how best to prepare for a hurricane. Some are lazy; others are "eternally optimistic" and never quite grasp the gravity of the danger. The losses are great for everyone, but especially for those who did not take reasonable measures to protect themselves from the ravages of the storm.

We must recognize that as long as we live on this sin-cursed planet with sinful people, we are going to encounter many storms. Wise people will prepare for those storms and will be able to weather them without great losses and, more importantly, without damage to the name and reputation of the God they claim to serve.

This study is very much like a "survival manual" for the times of trouble which inevitably will hit our lives. May this brief study better equip you to handle the storms of life to the glory of God.

WEEK 1

THE DANGER

THE GREATEST DANGER IS ALWAYS THE FLESH.

Memorize Galatians 5:16-17 this week.

Review it daily throughout the entire week and be prepared to write it from memory on Day 5.[1]

KJV

[16] This I say then, Walk in the Spirit, and ye shall not fulfil the lust of the flesh. [17] For the flesh lusteth against the Spirit, and the Spirit against the flesh: and these are contrary the one to the other: so that ye cannot do the things that ye would.

ESV

[16] But I say, walk by the Spirit, and you will not gratify the desires of the flesh. [17] For the desires of the flesh are against the Spirit, and the desires of the Spirit are against the flesh, for these are opposed to each other, to keep you from doing the things you want to do.

---

[1] If you already know Galatians 5:16-17 or wish to memorize additional passages, consider memorizing 1 Corinthians 10:13, James 1:12, or James 1:1-8.

❏ **TAKE TIME TO READ THE TEXT:**

Read chapter one, pages 1-10 of WTC.[2]

❏ **TAKE TIME TO REFLECT UPON THE TRUTH**

1. In the blanks below write the two statements in today's reading assignment that are the most significant to you. Be prepared to discuss why the statements you chose were significant to you.

    a.

    ____

    ____

    ____

    ____

---

[2] *WTC* refers to the text, *When Trouble Comes.*

b. ____

____

____

____

____

2. Review the eleven crisis situations listed on pages 4-6 of WTC. Then list the crisis situations which you face right now or suspect you will face within the near future.

____

____

3. Which crisis situation in the past was the scene of your biggest failure? Why?

____

____

____

4. Which crisis situation in the past was the scene of your biggest success? Why?

____

____

____

5. The word *lust* in the verse for this week simply means "strong desire." The context of the word determines whether the strong desire is good or bad. These verses teach that the desires of the

"flesh"—those generated by our sinful nature— are at war with those things the Spirit of God desires for us. When we indulge in the desires of our sinful flesh, we disobey the Spirit of God and damage our relationship with Jesus Christ.

What strong desires of your flesh—your sinful nature—keep you from walking in a close relationship with Jesus Christ? They can be attitudes, actions, or ambitions.

____

____

____

6. To "walk in the Spirit" means to listen to the conviction of God's Spirit through His Word and to obey Him. The result is that our "walk" or "lifestyle" reflects godly responses rather than fleshly reactions. Your text says, "[God] does not promise to deliver us from our negative circumstances, but He does promise to deliver us from the wrong responses—the dangers—that will destroy our joy and obscure His glory (1 Corinthians 10:13)" (WTC, 9-10).

If you were walking in the Spirit instead of walking after your flesh in the areas you listed in your answer above, what would your responses look like?

____

____

____

❑ TAKE TIME TO RENEW YOUR MIND

Memorize Galatians 5:16-17 this week. It is printed on page 1 of this study.

To build a relationship with God, you will need to respond to Him about the things you have learned from Him today. You can use the following helps as you P.R.A.Y.

PRAISE—Thank God for what He has done for you recently or shown you from His Word for which you can praise Him (Psalm 8; 1 Chronicles 29:11–13)?

____

____

REPENT—Tell God what you need to confess to Him and forsake (1 John 1:9; Psalm 32:1–5)?

____

____

ASK—Ask God to do things for you or someone else today (Matthew 7: 7–11; Hebrews 4:14–16)?

____

____

YIELD—Admit to God how you need to humble yourself to Him and give up something you are stubbornly holding on to (James 4:6–10)?

____

____

- Your text says, "Every test of life—every crisis—has within it a danger that we cannot "escape" if we respond wrongly and an opportunity to show how great God is if we respond correctly" (WTC, 2). This week ask God to make you increasingly conscious of that truth so that you can avoid the dangers of a wrong response and can show something of God to others by a correct response.

WEEK 1
THE DANGER

❑ **TAKE TIME TO READ THE TEXT**

Read chapter two, pages 11-18 of WTC.

❑ **TAKE TIME TO REFLECT UPON THE TRUTH**

1. In the blanks below write the two statements in today's reading
    assignment that are the most significant to you. Be prepared to
    discuss why the statements you chose were significant to you.

    a. ____

    ____

    ____

    ____

    ____

    b. ____

    ____

2. The text lists several fleshly ways that Peggy could have reacted to Bill's pornography. List several other fleshly responses she could have had.

3. Read Numbers 20:1-13. Check the box when you have finished reading the passage. Then answer the following questions from the passage. ❏

   a. What was the crisis facing the people of Israel in Numbers 20?

   b. Describe their sinful, fleshly response.

   c. What crisis did Moses face?

d. Describe Moses' sinful, fleshly response. __________________

e. How did Moses' sinful, fleshly response complicate an already
    bad situation?

f. What might Moses have been able to teach the people about
    God had he responded correctly?

g. What did God say was at the root of Moses' sinful response
    according to Numbers 20:12?

❑ **TAKE TIME TO RENEW YOUR MIND**

Memorize Galatians 5:16-17 this week.

❑ **TAKE TIME TO RESPOND TO GOD**

To build a relationship with God, you will need to respond to Him about the things you have learned from Him today.

PRAISE—Thank God for what He has done for you recently or shown you from His Word for which you can praise Him (Psalm 8; 1 Chronicles 29:11–13)?

____

____

REPENT—Tell God what you need to confess to Him and forsake (1 John 1:9; Psalm 32:1–5)?

____

____

ASK—Ask God to do things for you or someone else today (Matthew 7: 7–11; Hebrews 4:14–16)?

____

____

YIELD—Admit to God how you need to humble yourself to Him and give up something you are stubbornly holding on to (James 4:6–10)?

____

____

- Your text says, "Every test of life—every crisis—has within it a danger that we cannot "escape" if we respond wrongly and an opportunity to show how great God is if we respond correctly" (WTC, 2). This week ask God to make you increasingly conscious of that truth so that you can avoid the dangers of a wrong response and can show something of God to others by a correct response.

❏ **TAKE TIME TO REFLECT UPON THE TRUTH**

1. Read 2 Kings 5:1-14. Check the box when you have finished reading
    the passage. ❏
    Answer the following questions from the passage.

    a. What physical crisis was Naaman facing? _______________

    ____

    ____

    b. 1 Peter 5:5 describes a spiritual crisis we all face. How does
        1 Peter 5:5 also describe Namaan's most important crisis—his
        spiritual need?

    ____

    ____

    ____

2. According to 1 Peter 5:5 what is God's solution to our stubborn pride and the means whereby we can obtain God's grace—His divine help?

____

____

____

3. In what crises of life are you most prone to react stubbornly? Think of those areas where God, others, and your own conscience accuse you of being stubbornly self-centered. Here are some examples: I am stubborn when. . .

- My spouse suggests a better way to do something. I'd rather do it my own way.

- My parents set a curfew for me. I think that I am old enough to set my own schedule.

- My pastor questions me about the sin battle I have struggled with. I don't like to be held accountable for my life.

List at least 5 areas of similar stubbornness in your own life.

1. ____

____

____

2. ____

____

____

3. ____

____

____

4. ____

____

____

5. ____

____

____

❏ **TAKE TIME TO RENEW YOUR MIND**

Memorize Galatians 5:16-17 this week.

❏ **TAKE TIME TO RESPOND TO GOD**

To build a relationship with God, you will need to respond to Him about the things you have learned from Him today.

PRAISE—Thank God for what He has done for you recently or shown you from His Word for which you can praise Him (Psalm 8; 1 Chronicles 29:11–13)?

____

____

REPENT—Tell God what you need to confess to Him and forsake (1 John 1:9; Psalm 32:1–5)?

____

____

A**SK**—Ask God to do things for you or someone else today (Matthew 7: 7–11; Hebrews 4:14–16)?

____

____

Y**IELD**—Admit to God how you need to humble yourself to Him and give up something you are stubbornly holding on to (James 4:6–10)?

____

____

- Your text says, "Every test of life—every crisis—has within it a danger that we cannot "escape" if we respond wrongly and an opportunity to show how great God is if we respond correctly" (WTC, 2). This week ask God to make you increasingly conscious of that truth so that you can avoid the dangers of a wrong response and can show something of God to others by a correct response.

❑ **TAKE TIME TO REFLECT UPON THE TRUTH**

1. Read Romans 12:17-21. Check the box when you have finished reading the passage. ❑
   Answer the following questions from the passage.

   Verse seventeen tells us that we should never pay back evil for evil. That means that vengeance is never an option when someone wrongs us. Revenge only further "infects the wound." It brings more evil into the situation. We cannot win the war against evil by using evil as a weapon in the conflicts of life. Revenge can include more than fist-fights and name-calling. It can include things like these:

   - Punishing the offender with the "silent treatment"

   - Gossiping about the offender's faults and failures to others

   - Rebuking the offender in a spirit contrary to Galatians 6:1 and Matthew 7:3-5

   - Giving the offender a good "tongue-lashing" (i.e., using harsh, critical, or insensitive words)

- Treating the offender with scorn and contempt (i.e., blowing the horn at a person who cuts you off in traffic, scowling at the offender as you walk by him)

When someone wrongs you, in what ways are you tempted to pay back evil for evil?

____

____

____

2. In Bible times when an enemy was trying to scale the walls of a city, the enemy would often put ladders up the side of the walls in order to climb over them. Those defending the city from the inside would start large bonfires and throw the hot coals over the walls onto the heads of the enemies coming up the ladders. It was very effective in discouraging the enemy.

   This is the picture Paul is alluding to in Romans 12:20 when he says that overcoming evil with good is very effective in winning the war against evil just as throwing hot coals on the heads of the enemies was very effective in holding off the enemy advances.

   Bear in mind that the Paul is not teaching that we should find some way to hurt the one who has hurt us. We are to find some way to hurt the advance of evil into the situation by overcoming the evil with good.

   What "good" could Peggy bring into her crisis that would help "overcome [Bill's] evil with good"?

   ____

   ____

   ____

❑ **T**AKE **T**IME TO **R**ENEW **Y**OUR **M**IND

Memorize Galatians 5:16-17.

❑ **T**AKE **T**IME TO **R**ESPOND TO **G**OD

To build a relationship with God, you will need to respond to Him about the things you have learned from Him today.

PRAISE—Thank God for what He has done for you recently or shown you from His Word for which you can praise Him (Psalm 8; 1 Chronicles 29:11–13)?

____

____

REPENT—Tell God what you need to confess to Him and forsake (1 John 1:9; Psalm 32:1–5)?

____

____

ASK—Ask God to do things for you or someone else today (Matthew 7: 7–11; Hebrews 4:14–16)?

____

____

YIELD—Admit to God how you need to humble yourself to Him and give up something you are stubbornly holding on to (James 4:6–10)?

____

____

- Your text says, "Every test of life—every crisis—has within it a danger that we cannot "escape" if we respond wrongly and an opportunity to show how great God is if we respond correctly" (WTC, 2). This week ask God to make you increasingly conscious of that truth so that you can avoid the dangers of a wrong response and can show something of God to others by a correct response.

❏ **TAKE TIME TO REFLECT UPON THE TRUTH**

1. Read James 3:1-18. Check the box when you have finished reading the passage. ❏
    Answer the following questions from the passage.

    This passage contrasts godly responses with fleshly responses, especially as they pertain to the use of our tongues.

2. What characteristics of fleshly responses are given in the following verses?

    • Verse 5 ____

    • Verse 6 ____

    • Verse 8 ____

    • Verse 9 ____

    • Verse 10 _______________________________________

    • Verse 14 _______________________________________

    • Verse 16 _______________________________________

3. According to James 3:15 what is the source of the fleshly responses
    you just studied in the verses listed above? _______________________

    ____

    ____

4. What characteristics of spiritual responses are given in the
    following verses?

    • Verse 9 ____

    • Verse 13 ____

    ____

    • Verse 17 ____

    ____

    ____

    ____

    • Verse 18 ____

    ____

❏ **TAKE TIME TO RENEW YOUR MIND**

   Write Galatians 5:16-17 from memory.

   ____

   ____

   ____

   ____

❑ **Take Time to Respond to God**

To build a relationship with God, you will need to respond to Him about the things you have learned from Him today.

PRAISE—Thank God for what He has done for you recently or shown you from His Word for which you can praise Him (Psalm 8; 1 Chronicles 29:11–13)?

REPENT—Tell God what you need to confess to Him and forsake (1 John 1:9; Psalm 32:1–5)?

ASK—Ask God to do things for you or someone else today (Matthew 7: 7–11; Hebrews 4:14–16)?

YIELD—Admit to God how you need to humble yourself to Him and give up something you are stubbornly holding on to (James 4:6–10)?

- Your text says, "Every test of life—every crisis—has within it a danger that we cannot "escape" if we respond wrongly and an opportunity to show how great God is if we respond correctly" (WTC, 2). This week ask God to make you increasingly conscious of that truth so that you can avoid the dangers of a wrong response and can show something of God to others by a correct response.

❏ Take Time to Reorder Your Life

Considering this week's reflections, write below anything you need to begin to do differently in your life. List as well the person whom you will ask to hold you accountable for these changes.

____

____

____

____

WEEK TWO

THE DELIVERANCE

THE GOSPEL IS ALWAYS THE ANSWER.

Memorize Romans 8:31-32 this week. Review it daily throughout the entire week and be prepared to write it from memory on Day 5.[3]

KJV
[31] What shall we then say to these things? If God be for us, who can be against us? [32] He that spared not his own Son, but delivered him up for us all, how shall he not with him also freely give us all things?

ESV
[31] What then shall we say to these things? If God is for us, who can be against us? [32] He who did not spare his own Son but gave him up for us all, how will he not also with him graciously give us all things?

---

[3]   If you already know Romans 8:31-32 or wish to memorize additional passsages, consider memorizing Matthew 16:24-26, Titus 2:11-12, or Romans 8:35-39.

WEEK 2
THE DELIVERANCE

❑ **TAKE TIME TO READ THE TEXT:**

Read chapter three, pages 19-27 of WTC.

❑ **TAKE TIME TO REFLECT UPON THE TRUTH**

1. In the blanks below write the two statements in today's reading
    assignment that are the most significant to you. Be prepared to
    discuss why the statements you chose were significant to you.

    a. ____

    ____

    ____

    ____

    ____

    b. ____

    ____

    ____

2. According to your reading in WTC, what is the biggest crisis a man can face?

____

3. How would you answer the following question presented in your reading for today? "If you were to die today from a terminal illness or in some tragic accident and you were to stand before God, how would you answer God when He asked you this question: 'Why should I let you into My heaven?'" (WTC, 21)

____

____

4. Some people feel that God should let them into heaven because they have lived sacrificial lives or have lived by a high moral standard. What does Titus 3:5 say about the ability of these "works of righteousness" to gain us entrance into heaven?

____

____

5. Eternal life is not a reward for living a good life since all men are sinners and are sentenced to eternal death for their sin, according to Romans 3:23 and Romans 6:23. What does 1 John 5:11-12 say we must have to be assured that we have eternal life?

6. According to Romans 10:9-10, what is required for a man to be able to have eternal salvation?

____

7. Can you confidently say that you have eternal life because you have trusted Jesus Christ as your personal sin substitute and you now have a personal relationship with Him because His Spirit lives in you? ____

❏ Take Time to Renew Your Mind

Memorize Romans 8:31-32.

❏ Take Time to Respond to God

To build a relationship with God, you will need to respond to Him about the things you have learned from Him today.

PRAISE—Thank God for what He has done for you recently or shown you from His Word for which you can praise Him (Psalm 8; 1 Chronicles 29:11–13)?

____

____

REPENT—Tell God what you need to confess to Him and forsake (1 John 1:9; Psalm 32:1–5)?

____

____

ASK—Ask God to do things for you or someone else today (Matthew 7: 7–11; Hebrews 4:14–16)?

____

____

Y**IELD**—Admit to God how you need to humble yourself to Him and give up something you are stubbornly holding on to (James 4:6–10)?

____

____

- If you do not have a personal relationship with Jesus Christ, you can have that today by praying a prayer to Jesus Christ like the one written out for you on page 26 of WTC.

- If you are already a born-again believer, thank God that He sent someone to you with the good news that Jesus Christ came to seek and to save that which was lost—and that He found you!

WEEK 2
THE DELIVERANCE

❑ **TAKE TIME TO READ THE TEXT:**

Read chapter four, pages 29-38 of WTC.

❑ **TAKE TIME TO REFLECT UPON THE TRUTH**

1. In the blanks below write the two statements in today's reading
    assignment that are the most significant to you. Be prepared to
    discuss why the statements you chose were significant to you.

    a.

    ____

    ____

    ____

    ____

    b.

    ____

    ____

    ____

2. In the section entitled, "Live the Christian Life the Same Way You Got It," your text said, "The gospel reveals man's condition. . . . The Bible teaches us that we still have within us the bent to live selfishly—to think of ourselves first. This inclination to think of ourselves first seems overwhelming at times—especially if we are in great pain" (WTC, 31).

In our study together last week, we looked at the danger of this fleshly nature from many angles. We will not expand on it further here, but we must keep in mind this sinful tendency if we are to appreciate that "the gospel reveals God's provision" (WTC, 31).

God knew that life on a fallen planet would be extremely hard for us. One day He will destroy this earth after transporting all of His redeemed children to be with Him. Until that time He has made some very powerful provisions for us so that we do not have to be consumed by evil when we are in a crisis.

Just as Jesus Christ is God's provision for our eternal salvation, He is also the provision for us when we face temporal trouble. The memory passage for this week, Romans 8:31-32, is very clear about this. Put the truths of these two verses in your own words.

Here is a powerful yet often overlooked comfort for God's people. He loves us! Believers who do not have a God-taught sense of this truth will often feel overwhelmed and alone in their troubled times. We shall look at God's love again in tomorrow's study.

❏ **Take Time to Renew Your Mind**

Memorize Romans 8:31-32.

❏ **Take Time to Respond to God**

To build a relationship with God, you will need to respond to Him about the things you have learned from Him today.

PRAISE—Thank God for what He has done for you recently or shown you from His Word for which you can praise Him (Psalm 8; 1 Chronicles 29:11–13)?

____

____

REPENT—Tell God what you need to confess to Him and forsake (1 John 1:9; Psalm 32:1–5)?

____

____

ASK—Ask God to do things for you or someone else today (Matthew 7: 7–11; Hebrews 4:14–16)?

____

____

YIELD—Admit to God how you need to humble yourself to Him and give up something you are stubbornly holding on to (James 4:6–10)?

____

____

- Today ask God to give you a fresh understanding and appreciation for what it means that He loves you. It will be a major source of stability when the times of pressure come.

DAY 3

WEEK 2
THE DELIVERANCE

❑ **TAKE TIME TO REFLECT UPON THE TRUTH**

Read Romans 8:35-39. Check the box when you have finished reading the passage. ❑
Answer the following questions from the passage.

1. Why do you think Paul had to remind us about God's love when we are facing trials?

____

____

____

2. Describe a time of difficulty when you were tempted to doubt God's love.

____

____

____

____

3. In Psalm 18 David is facing a crisis. He is being chased by King Saul who intends to put David to death. This psalm is David's account of his deliverance. Read Psalm 18:1-19. Check the box when you have finished reading the passage. ❏ Then answer the following questions from the passage.

In verse 19 David gave the reason that the Lord delivered Him. What is that reason?

____

4. Would you say that the Lord has the same "delight" in you? Explain your answer.

____

____

____

____

❏ **Take Time to Renew Your Mind**

Memorize Romans 8:31-32.

❏ **Take Time to Respond to God**

To build a relationship with God, you will need to respond to Him about the things you have learned from Him today.

PRAISE—Thank God for what He has done for you recently or shown you from His Word for which you can praise Him (Psalm 8; 1 Chronicles 29:11–13)?

____

____

R EPENT—Tell God what you need to confess to Him and forsake (1 John 1:9; Psalm 32:1–5)?

____

____

A SK—Ask God to do things for you or someone else today (Matthew 7: 7–11; Hebrews 4:14–16)?

____

____

Y IELD—Admit to God how you need to humble yourself to Him and give up something you are stubbornly holding on to (James 4:6–10)?

____

____

- Today continue to ask God to give you a fresh understanding and appreciation for what it means that He loves you. It will be a major source of stability when the pressure times come.

❑ **TAKE TIME TO REFLECT UPON THE TRUTH**

1. Read Hebrews 11:1-40. Check the box when you have finished reading the passage. ❑
   Answer the following questions from the passage.

   Hebrews 11 is God's "Hall of Faith." In it He shows us the kind of people who please Him. The chapter lists many familiar Bible heroes—Noah, Abraham, Joseph, and Moses. But it also speaks of a host of nameless "heroes," many of whom lost their lives for their godly testimony.

2. According to Hebrews 11:35 what sustained Moses during his times of difficulty? _______________________________

   ____

3. What application does that have for you? _______________

   ____

   ____

4. Having "faith" just means that even in the midst of trouble we do not turn our eyes away from God. Some people think that if they can acquire enough of this thing called "faith" they can cash it in to God for the deliverance they want from their problems. Faith, however, is "the gaze of the soul upon a saving God."[4] When we "have faith," we do not let the distractions of our trials cause us to forget God's purposes for us nor His provisions for us during these times. How well do you keep your focus on God's purposes and provisions during times of trouble?

____

____

____

5. No one can keep his "gaze . . . upon the saving God" if he is not spending much daily time in the Word of God. God uses the Bible, His inspired Word, to instruct us about Himself and to remind us of our responsibilities to Him. This is the message of Romans 10:17, which says, "so then faith cometh by hearing, and hearing by the word of God." It is important that you not miss the direct connection between a believer's ability to handle trials well and the quality of the relationship he has with God through His Word. If you are honest with yourself, what part does the Word of God have in your daily life?

____

____

____

❏ **Take Time to Renew Your Mind**

Memorize Romans 8:31-32.

---

4   A. W. Tozer, *The Pursuit of God* (Camp Hill, Pa.: Christian Publications, 1982), 81.

To build a relationship with God, you will need to respond to Him about the things you have learned from Him today.

PRAISE—Thank God for what He has done for you recently or shown you from His Word for which you can praise Him (Psalm 8; 1 Chronicles 29:11–13)?

____

____

REPENT—Tell God what you need to confess to Him and forsake (1 John 1:9; Psalm 32:1–5)?

____

____

ASK—Ask God to do things for you or someone else today (Matthew 7: 7–11; Hebrews 4:14–16)?

____

____

YIELD—Admit to God how you need to humble yourself to Him and give up something you are stubbornly holding on to (James 4:6–10)?

____

____

- Today ask God to help you see Him more clearly in His Word as you read it and study it every day. Remember, your confidence— your faith—in who God is and what He is like cannot grow without daily, reflective time in the Word.

THE DELIVERANCE

❏ **TAKE TIME TO REFLECT UPON THE TRUTH**

1. Read again Tim Mahler's testimony on pages 33-36 of WTC. Check the box when you have finished the reading. ❏

    What encouraged you most about Tim's testimony? ___________

    ____

    ____

2. Read again the prayer on pages 37-38 of WTC. Check the box when you have finished the reading. ❏

    Can you say that this prayer is the testimony of your heart? _______

    If it is not a reality to you at this time, what is keeping you from turning to God in this way?

    ____

    ____

    ____

    ____

If it is the prayer of your heart, what difference is it making in the way you have handled problems recently?

____

____

____

____

❏ **Take Time to Renew Your Mind**

Write Romans 8:31-32 from memory.

____

____

____

____

____

____

❏ **Take Time to Respond to God**

To build a relationship with God, you will need to respond to Him about the things you have learned from Him today.

PRAISE—Thank God for what He has done for you recently or shown you from His Word for which you can praise Him (Psalm 8; 1 Chronicles 29:11–13)?

REPENT—Tell God what you need to confess to Him and forsake (1 John 1:9; Psalm 32:1–5)?

ASK—Ask God to do things for you or someone else today (Matthew 7: 7–11; Hebrews 4:14–16)?

YIELD—Admit to God how you need to humble yourself to Him and give up something you are stubbornly holding on to (James 4:6–10)?

- Today continue to ask God to give you a fresh understanding and appreciation that He loves you enough to deliver you. It will be a major source of stability when the pressure times come.

❑ **TAKE TIME TO REORDER YOUR LIFE**

Considering this week's reflections, write below anything you need to begin to do differently in your life. List as well the person whom you will ask to hold you accountable for these changes.

____

____

____

____

____

____

THE DISPLAY

GOD'S GLORY IS ALWAYS THE GOAL.

Memorize Matthew 5:16 this week. Review it daily throughout the entire week and be prepared to write it from memory on Day 5.[5]

KJV

Let your light so shine before men, that they may see your good works, and glorify your Father which is in heaven.

ESV

In the same way, let your light shine before others, so that they may see your good works and give glory to your Father who is in heaven.

---

5   If you already know Matthew 5:16 or wish to memorize additional passsages, consider memorizing 1 Corinthians 6:19-20, 1 Corinthians 10:31, or 2 Corinthians 4:5-11.

❑ **TAKE TIME TO READ THE TEXT:**

Read chapter five, pages 39-49 of WTC.

❑ **TAKE TIME TO REFLECT UPON THE TRUTH**

1. In the blanks below write the two statements in today's reading assignment that are most significant to you. Be prepared to discuss why the statements you chose were significant to you.

   a. ____

   ____

   ____

   ____

   b. ____

   ____

   ____

2. The phrase "glorifying God" means that we show in some way through our decisions that God is first place in our lives. He is first in priority and importance. No one deserves as much honor and respect as the Creator of all things. He is also first in all of His attributes. No one has more love, more patience, more power, more wisdom, more faithfulness, and more compassion than the Creator God of the Bible.

    Those of us who have tasted His wonderful goodness and have seen His overwhelming greatness desire to give Him the credit He deserves in every decision we make. This is what Paul meant when he said, "Whether therefore ye eat or drink, or whatsoever ye do, do all to the glory of God" (I Corinthians 10:31). In other words, no matter what circumstance you find yourself in, make decisions that show that God is first.

    If you are honest with yourself, how much does "glorifying God"—making sure that He is shown to be first—matter to you in the daily decisions you make? Rate yourself in the areas listed below, using the following scale.

    1-strongly agree; 2-agree; 3-somewhat agree; 4-slightly disagree; 5-strongly disagree

    _______ I daily spend time in God's Word so that by knowing Him better my confidence in Him can grow and I can more easily put Him first.

    _______ I readily turn to God in prayer when I face troubled times because if I do not quickly submit to Him and His ways in my crisis, I will eventually make a fleshly response.

_______ I want others to know that God is first, and I regularly witness of His salvation to those around me who are lost.

_______ I show that God is first through the use of my money and time. I do not squander it on my own interests but consciously seek to advance His kingdom by the way I use these resources.

_______ When I receive undeserved wrong from someone else, I make it my primary goal to reach that person's heart so that his relationship with me and with God can be restored.

_______ I am conscious that my personal integrity and God's reputation are at stake in the manner in which I carry out my responsibilities at my employment and at home. I, therefore, seek to maintain a Christian testimony that is above reproach in these areas.

_______ I know that to walk in the Spirit I must not "make any provision for the flesh" in my life and, therefore, I am very cautious about the amount and the kinds of entertainment and recreation which I pursue.

How would you summarize your overall concern for the glory of God, based upon your responses to these biblical responsibilities?

____

____

____

____

❏ **T**AKE **T**IME TO **R**ENEW **Y**OUR **M**IND

Memorize Matthew 5:16.

❏ **T**AKE **T**IME TO **R**ESPOND TO **G**OD

To build a relationship with God, you will need to respond to Him about the things you have learned from Him today.

PRAISE—Thank God for what He has done for you recently or shown you from His Word for which you can praise Him (Psalm 8; 1 Chronicles 29:11–13)?

____

____

REPENT—Tell God what you need to confess to Him and forsake (1 John 1:9; Psalm 32:1–5)?

____

____

ASK—Ask God to do things for you or someone else today (Matthew 7: 7–11; Hebrews 4:14–16)?

____

____

YIELD—Admit to God how you need to humble yourself to Him and give up something you are stubbornly holding on to (James 4:6–10)?

____

____

- Today ask God to make you sensitive to the events in your daily life which give you the opportunity to show that God is first. Also ask Him for the grace to deny yourself in those situations so that you do not put yourself first.

WEEK 3
THE DISPLAY

❑ **TAKE TIME TO REFLECT UPON THE TRUTH**

1. Read Daniel 3:1-30. Check the box when you have finished reading the passage. ❑

   Answer the following questions from the passage.

2. What choices did the Hebrews make that showed that God was first?

   ____

   ____

   ____

3. What other choices could they have made that would have shown they were thinking of themselves first?

   ____

   ____

   ____

4. What effect did their choice to show that God is first have on other people?

____

____

____

5. List at least five choices you have faced within the past two days when you could make decisions that showed that either God was first or you were first in your life.

a. _______________________________________

____

b. _______________________________________

____

c. _______________________________________

____

❑ **TAKE TIME TO RENEW YOUR MIND**

Memorize Matthew 5:16.

❑ **TAKE TIME TO RESPOND TO GOD**

To build a relationship with God, you will need to respond to Him about the things you have learned from Him today.

PRAISE—Thank God for what He has done for you recently or shown you from His Word for which you can praise Him (Psalm 8; 1 Chronicles 29:11–13)?

____

____

REPENT—Tell God what you need to confess to Him and forsake (1 John 1:9; Psalm 32:1–5)?

ASK—Ask God to do things for you or someone else today (Matthew 7: 7–11; Hebrews 4:14–16)?

YIELD—Admit to God how you need to humble yourself to Him and give up something you are stubbornly holding on to (James 4:6–10)?

- Today ask God to make you sensitive to the events in your daily life which give you the opportunity to show that God is first. Also ask Him for the grace to deny yourself in those situations so that you do not put yourself first.

❏ **Take Time to Read the Text:**

Read chapter six, pages 51-59 of WTC.

❏ **Take Time to Reflect Upon the Truth**

1. In the blanks below write the two statements in today's reading assignment that are most significant to you. Be prepared to discuss why the statements you chose were significant to you.

   a.

   ____

   ____

   ____

   ____

   b. ____

   ____

   ____

____

____

2. Your reading for today lists two reasons people say, "I have a hard
    time trusting God." What are those two reasons?

    a. _____________________________________

    ____

    ____

    b. _____________________________________

    ____

    ____

3. According to your reading today, why could we say that every
    decision is a trust decision?

    ____

    ____

    ____

❏ **TAKE TIME TO RENEW YOUR MIND**

Memorize Matthew 5:16.

❏ **TAKE TIME TO RESPOND TO GOD**

To build a relationship with God, you will need to respond to Him
about the things you have learned from Him today.

PRAISE—Thank God for what He has done for you recently or shown you from His Word for which you can praise Him (Psalm 8; 1 Chronicles 29:11–13)?

____

____

REPENT—Tell God what you need to confess to Him and forsake (1 John 1:9; Psalm 32:1–5)?

____

____

ASK—Ask God to do things for you or someone else today (Matthew 7: 7–11; Hebrews 4:14–16)?

____

____

YIELD—Admit to God how you need to humble yourself to Him and give up something you are stubbornly holding on to (James 4:6–10)?

____

____

- Today ask God to make you more and more aware that your every decision reveals who it is you trust most—God or yourself. Be sure to ask forgiveness for those decisions in which you revealed that you trusted yourself most. Those decisions glorified you—put you first and robbed God of His glory.

❑ **TAKE TIME TO REFLECT UPON THE TRUTH**

1. Read 2 Chronicles 14:1-15. Check the box when you have finished reading the passage. ❑
   Answer the following questions from the passage.

2. Asa was the King of Judah, and though his kingdom enjoyed ten years of relative peace, he eventually faced a formidable foe of a million Ethiopians. What choices did Asa make, both in his ten years of peace and in his preparation for battle, that showed he was thoroughly convinced that showing God to be first was his primary mission as king? List several.

____

____

____

____

____

____

3. Read 2 Chronicles 16:1-10. Check the box when you have finished reading the passage. ❑ Then answer the following questions from the passage.

4. Asa was faced again with a time of trouble. This time an army from the northern kingdom, Israel, invaded the southern kingdom, Judah. What choices did Asa make this time that revealed he was no longer putting God first in his thinking?

____

____

____

____

____

❑ **TAKE TIME TO RENEW YOUR MIND**

Memorize Matthew 5:16.

❑ **TAKE TIME TO RESPOND TO GOD**

To build a relationship with God, you will need to respond to Him about the things you have learned from Him today.

PRAISE—Thank God for what He has done for you recently or shown you from His Word for which you can praise Him (Psalm 8; 1 Chronicles 29:11–13)?

____

____

REPENT—Tell God what you need to confess to Him and forsake (1 John 1:9; Psalm 32:1–5)?

____

____

A**SK**—Ask God to do things for you or someone else today (Matthew 7: 7–11; Hebrews 4:14–16)?

____

____

Y**IELD**—Admit to God how you need to humble yourself to Him and give up something you are stubbornly holding on to (James 4:6–10)?

____

____

- Again today ask God to make you sensitive to the events in your daily life which give you the opportunity to show that God is first. Keep in mind the lessons you learned from Asa's life today. It is easy for us to make the wrong choices as Asa did, even after years of right choices.

WEEK 3
THE DISPLAY

❑ **TAKE TIME TO REFLECT UPON THE TRUTH**

1. Read 2 Corinthians 4:7-18. Check the box when you have finished reading the passage. ❑
   Answer the following questions from the passage.

2. In verses 8-9 of the passage you just read, the apostle Paul speaks of the troubles he encountered in the ministry. Summarize what he is saying in these two verses.

   ____

   ____

   ____

   ____

3. Paul says in verses 16-18 that he does not faint under the weight of the trouble he has experienced and then testifies of what sustains him during troubled times. What does he say is the secret to his endurance?

4. Do you have a God-enabled endurance in the troubles of life which comes from genuinely looking "at the things which are not seen"?

____

____

5. If not, what would you say is keeping you from this kind of experience in your Christian life?

____

____

____

6. God promises in these verses that you will have a God-enabled endurance if you are regularly seeking the things which are not seen and which are eternal. For an extended study on this topic read *Created for His Glory* by Jim Berg (Greenville, SC: Bob Jones University Press, 2002). It is an extended study of the realities of our great God, which the believer must know in order to be stable in times of uncertainty.

❏ **TAKE TIME TO RENEW YOUR MIND**

Write Matthew 5:16 from memory.

____

____

____

____

____

❏ **Take Time to Respond to God**

To build a relationship with God, you will need to respond to Him about the things you have learned from Him today.

PRAISE—Thank God for what He has done for you recently or shown you from His Word for which you can praise Him (Psalm 8; 1 Chronicles 29:11–13)?

____

____

REPENT—Tell God what you need to confess to Him and forsake (1 John 1:9; Psalm 32:1–5)?

____

____

ASK—Ask God to do things for you or someone else today (Matthew 7: 7–11; Hebrews 4:14–16)?

____

____

YIELD—Admit to God how you need to humble yourself to Him and give up something you are stubbornly holding on to (James 4:6–10)?

____

____

- Today make a commitment to God that you want to pursue the "things which are above" (Colossians 3:1), rather than setting so much of your attention on earthly things, so that you can have the God-enabled endurance which He wants you to have during times of trouble.

❏ Take Time to Reorder Your Life

Considering this week's reflections, write below anything you need to begin to do differently in your life. List as well the person whom you will ask to hold you accountable for these changes.

____

____

____

____

THE DELIGHT

GOD HIMSELF IS ALWAYS ENOUGH.

Memorize Isaiah 41:10 this week. Review it daily throughout the entire week and be prepared to write it from memory on Day 5.[6]

KJV
Fear thou not; for I am with thee: be not dismayed; for I am thy God: I will strengthen thee; yea, I will help thee; yea, I will uphold thee with the right hand of my righteousness.

ESV
Fear not, for I am with you; be not dismayed, for I am your God; I will strengthen you, I will help you, I will uphold you with my righteous right hand.

---

6   If you already know Isaiah 41:10 or wish to memorize additional passsages, consider memorizing Isaiah 40:27-31, Psalm 121, or

Psalm 16:8-9, 11.

❑ **TAKE TIME TO READ THE TEXT:**

Read chapter seven, pages 61-69 of WTC.

❑ **TAKE TIME TO REFLECT UPON THE TRUTH**

1. In the blanks below write the two statements in today's reading assignment that are most significant to you. Be prepared to discuss why the statements you chose were significant to you.

   a.

____

____

____

____

   b. _________________________________

____

____

2. Your reading today included the statement, "When there are things that you do not know about your life's situation, you must focus on the things that you do know about your God" (WTC, 63). Think for a few moments about a crisis or problem you are currently facing. In your own wisdom you might be tempted to think that if you only had the answer to certain things related to your crisis, you could be at peace. What are those things you feel would give you peace if you knew them?

____

____

____

3. Remember the story "Courage to Face a Bully" on pages 64-65 of WTC? The relief for my daughter's unrest did not come because the bully went away but rather because she knew her father—who cared about her—was present. What does this tell you that we need to know about God for our hearts to rest?

____

____

❑ **TAKE TIME TO RENEW YOUR MIND**

Memorize Isaiah 41:10.

❑ **TAKE TIME TO RESPOND TO GOD**

To build a relationship with God, you will need to respond to Him about the things you have learned from Him today.

PRAISE—Thank God for what He has done for you recently or shown you from His Word for which you can praise Him (Psalm 8; 1 Chronicles 29:11–13)?

REPENT—Tell God what you need to confess to Him and forsake (1 John 1:9; Psalm 32:1–5)?

ASK—Ask God to do things for you or someone else today (Matthew 7: 7–11; Hebrews 4:14–16)?

YIELD—Admit to God how you need to humble yourself to Him and give up something you are stubbornly holding on to (James 4:6–10)?

- If your spirit has been filled with worry, doubt, fears, and discouragements, you need to ask God to forgive you for your unbelief. Ask Him as well to teach you more of Himself as you meditate upon portions of His Word which acquaint you with who He is. You must spend much time inspecting His "squad car" if you are going to feel safe with Him.

DAY 2

WEEK 4
THE DELIGHT

❑ **TAKE TIME TO REFLECT UPON THE TRUTH**

1. Read Psalm 103. Check the box when you have finished reading the passage. ❑ Then answer the following questions from the passage.

2. In Psalm 103:1-2 David reminds us to give thanks to God and forget not all His blessings—His benefits—to us. What "benefits" from God are listed in this Psalm? Find ten and put them into your own words below; do not just copy down the words out of your Bible. Think through what David is saying about God and His work on our behalf.

c. ____

d. ____

e. ____

f. ____

g. ____

h. ____

i. ____

j. ______________________________

k. ______________________________

l. ______________________________

❏ **TAKE TIME TO RENEW YOUR MIND**

Memorize Isaiah 41:10.

❏ **TAKE TIME TO RESPOND TO GOD**

To build a relationship with God, you will need to respond to Him about the things you have learned from Him today.

PRAISE—Thank God for what He has done for you recently or shown you from His Word for which you can praise Him (Psalm 8; 1 Chronicles 29:11–13)?

____

____

REPENT—Tell God what you need to confess to Him and forsake (1 John 1:9; Psalm 32:1–5)?

____

____

ASK—Ask God to do things for you or someone else today (Matthew 7: 7–11; Hebrews 4:14–16)?

____

____

YIELD—Admit to God how you need to humble yourself to Him and give up something you are stubbornly holding on to (James 4:6–10)?

____

____

- Ask God to make you aware of the "benefits" He has sent your way in His goodness. Spend time praising Him for His kindness to you in these ways.

❏ **Take Time to Reflect Upon the Truth**

1. Page 66 of WTC states that "God is unlimited in His power." Look up each of the references listed in the book for that characteristic of God. In addition read Isaiah 40:9-26. Check the box when you have finished reading the passages. ❏
   Answer the following questions from what you have read.

2. What did you learn from these passages about the characteristics of God's power?

   ____

   ____

   ____

3. What did you learn about God's power that should be a comfort to you when trouble comes?

   ____

   ____

   ____

4. What sinful responses do you make in the face of trouble because
    you forget that God is unlimited in His power?

____

____

____

❏ TAKE TIME TO RENEW YOUR MIND

Memorize Isaiah 41:10.

❏ TAKE TIME TO RESPOND TO GOD

To build a relationship with God, you will need to respond to Him
about the things you have learned from Him today.

PRAISE—Thank God for what He has done for you recently or
shown you from His Word for which you can praise Him (Psalm 8;
1 Chronicles 29:11–13)?

____

____

REPENT—Tell God what you need to confess to Him and
forsake (1 John 1:9; Psalm 32:1–5)?

____

____

ASK—Ask God to do things for you or someone else today
(Matthew 7: 7–11; Hebrews 4:14–16)?

____

____

YIELD—Admit to God how you need to humble yourself to Him
and give up something you are stubbornly holding on to
(James 4:6–10)?

____

____

- Ask God to show you clearly His power that He will use on your behalf to rescue you from the danger of your flesh during a crisis.

❏ **TAKE TIME TO REFLECT UPON THE TRUTH**

1. Page 66 of WTC states that "God is unlimited in His wisdom." Look up each of the references listed in the book for that characteristic of God. In addition read I Corinthians 1:23-31. Check the box when you have finished reading the passages. ❏ Answer the following questions from what you have read.

2. What did you learn from these passages about the characteristics of God's wisdom?

____

____

____

3. What did you learn about God's wisdom that should be a comfort to you when trouble comes?

____

____

____

4. What sinful responses do you make in the face of trouble because you forget that God is unlimited in His wisdom?

____

____

❑ **TAKE TIME TO RENEW YOUR MIND**

Memorize Isaiah 41:10.

❑ **TAKE TIME TO RESPOND TO GOD**

To build a relationship with God, you will need to respond to Him about the things you have learned from Him today.

PRAISE—Thank God for what He has done for you recently or shown you from His Word for which you can praise Him (Psalm 8; 1 Chronicles 29:11–13)?

____

____

REPENT—Tell God what you need to confess to Him and forsake (1 John 1:9; Psalm 32:1–5)?

____

____

ASK—Ask God to do things for you or someone else today (Matthew 7: 7–11; Hebrews 4:14–16)?

____

____

YIELD—Admit to God how you need to humble yourself to Him and give up something you are stubbornly holding on to (James 4:6–10)?

____

____

- Ask God to show you clearly His wisdom that He will use on your behalf to rescue you from the danger of your flesh during a crisis.

❏ **T**AKE **T**IME TO **R**EFLECT **U**PON THE **T**RUTH

1. Page 66 of WTC states that "God is unlimited in His love." Look up each of the references listed in the book for that characteristic of God. In addition read Romans 8:31-39 again. You read it in an earlier lesson too. Check the box when you have finished reading the passages ❏
Answer the following questions from what you have read.

2. What did you learn from these passages about the characteristics of God's love?

____

____

____

____

3. What did you learn—or of what were you reminded—about God's love that should be a comfort to you when trouble comes?

____

____

____

4. What sinful responses do you make in the face of trouble because you forget that God is unlimited in His love for you?

____

____

____

❏ **TAKE TIME TO RENEW YOUR MIND**

Write Isaiah 41:10 from memory.

____

____

____

____

____

____

❏ **TAKE TIME TO RESPOND TO GOD**

To build a relationship with God, you will need to respond to Him about the things you have learned from Him today.

$\mathbf{P}$RAISE—Thank God for what He has done for you recently or shown you from His Word for which you can praise Him (Psalm 8; 1 Chronicles 29:11–13)?

$\mathbf{R}$EPENT—Tell God what you need to confess to Him and forsake (1 John 1:9; Psalm 32:1–5)?

$\mathbf{A}$SK—Ask God to do things for you or someone else today (Matthew 7: 7–11; Hebrews 4:14–16)?

$\mathbf{Y}$IELD—Admit to God how you need to humble yourself to Him and give up something you are stubbornly holding on to (James 4:6–10)?

- Ask God to show you clearly His wisdom that He will use on your behalf to rescue you from the danger of your flesh during a crisis.

❏ **TAKE TIME TO REORDER YOUR LIFE**

Considering this week's reflections, write below anything you need to begin to do differently in your life. List as well the person whom you will ask to hold you accountable for these changes.